Aunt Fanny

**The Orphan's Home Mittens**

The sixth and last Book of the Series

Aunt Fanny

**The Orphan's Home Mittens**
*The sixth and last Book of the Series*

ISBN/EAN: 9783744662550

Printed in Europe, USA, Canada, Australia, Japan

Cover: Foto ©Thomas Meinert / pixelio.de

More available books at **www.hansebooks.com**

Tent where George went to Church.

Willie's Portrait of Jeff. Davis.

THE
# ORPHAN'S HOME MITTENS;

AND

GEORGE'S ACCOUNT OF THE

## BATTLE OF ROANOKE ISLAND.

BEING

THE SIXTH AND LAST BOOK OF THE SERIES.

BY

AUNT FANNY

AUTHOR OF THE SIX NIGHTCAP BOOKS, ETC.

NEW YORK:
D. APPLETON AND COMPANY,
443 & 445 BROADWAY.
LONDON: 16 LITTLE BRITAIN.
1863.

Entered, according to Act of Congress, in the year 1862, by
FANNY BARROW,
In the Clerk's Office of the District Court of the United States for the Southern District of New York.

I DEDICATE THIS BOOK

TO MY DEAR LITTLE

# LIZZIE WAINWRIGHT,

THE GRANDDAUGHTER OF

A FAITHFUL AND VALIANT SOLDIER OF CHRIST.

THE DAUGHTER OF

A LOYAL AND BRAVE NAVAL OFFICER,

AND THE NIECE OF

A FRIEND I RESPECT AND LOVE.

# CONTENTS.

                                            PAGE

THE ORPHAN'S HOME; in which is introduced "NEW YEAR'S RESOLUTIONS" and "THE MINISTER'S STORY,"   7

THE BATTLE OF ROANOKE ISLAND, . . . 96

THE LAST OF THE MITTENS, . . . . 127

MISS SECESH, . . . . . . . . 134

# THE ORPHAN'S HOME.

It was now the second week in January, 1862. One evening, Aunt Fanny came to see the children. In an instant, she was surrounded, and hugged, and squeezed, and kissed, till she was certain they had loved a pound or two off her weight; but then they put it on again before she left, by making her laugh so at their capers and talk, that she said she thought she could feel the fat growing; so that made it all square and comfortable.

"I read such a charming little poem in the 'Independent' some weeks ago," said Aunt Fanny.

"Tell it to us! we want to hear it!" cried the children.

"How do you suppose I can remember seven long verses? I do recollect one or two, but that is because I suspect the writer had you children in his eye when he wrote them.

"Oh, Aunt Fanny!" said little Willie, in a reproachful tone, "we didn't get into the poor man's eye. You ought to be ashamed to tell such a story!"

Such shouts of laughter greeted this speech, that an old lady next door, hearing them through the walls, and thinking they were cheers, put on her spectacles, and hobbled to the window, expecting to see a torchlight procession—but poor little Willie, after wondering a moment, with his mouth wide open, what it all meant, rushed up to his mother, and hiding his face in her lap, began to cry.

"Never mind, dear," she said, kissing him; "Aunt Fanny meant that the man was *thinking* about you when he wrote the poetry. Of course, she knows my little Willie wouldn't poke through anybody's eye, to see what he had behind it. Aunt Fanny made use of what is called a 'figure of speech.' Don't cry any more."

Then all the children coaxed him, and kissed him, and made the kitten Mary O'Reilly kiss him, at which he burst out laughing, and felt quite happy again.

The crochet needles twinkled and twitched faster than ever, as Aunt Fanny repeated these lines:

" Knit—knit—knit—
If you've patriot blood in your veins!
Knit—knit—knit—
For our boys on Southern plains.
Our boys on Southern hills,
Our boys on Southern vales,
By the woods and streams of Dixie's Land,
Are feeling the wintry gales.

" Knit—knit—knit—
The socks, and mittens, and gloves!

Knit—knit—knit—
Each one that her country loves!
The mittens with finger and thumb complete,
The gloves for the drummers their drums to beat,
And the nice warm socks for the shivering feet,
Knit—knit—knit!"

"Is that all you can remember? Oh, how good it is!" cried the children.

"Suppose I make a verse?" said the little mother.

"Oh, do! do! they all entreated.

"Well, here it is:

"And if you can't knit—crochèt!*
The mittens with finger and thumb,
The old ones can finish a pair in a day,
And the children each make one.
For George, and his comrades brave,
Who have gone our country to save,
Will work heart and hand, till we make Dixie's land
Repent for her sins, and behave!"

The children thought this a capital verse, and Johnny came very near ex-

* Pronounced croshày.

claiming, " Bully for you." Very luckily, he recollected himself in time, for his mother would have sent him to bed in " double quick," if he had uttered this vulgar, slang expression.

"I had a talk with my ten naughty boys to day," said Aunt Fanny.

" Why, where in the world did you find so many together?" cried Harry. Who ever heard of such a quantity of bad children in a bunch?

" I ought to have said," she answered, " that they were reported to me some time ago, as being very bad; but I did not find them so dreadful as I expected; besides which, my heart softened to them, and I made excuses for them to myself, because they are all orphans."

" Then it must have been at the Orphan's Home," cried the children, for they knew Aunt Fanny was one of the managers.

"Yes, it was there; and I believe I will write a little history of how there came to be this Home for Orphans; and you can work it up in your mittens.

"Oh, yes, do! how long will it take you? We'll write to George that these mittens have listened, with their fingers and thumbs for ears, to your "Orphan's Home" story. They will be the most interesting mittens of all: more so, than those we got by our little play."

The children wished George had ears a hundred miles long, so he could hear all these wonderful and charming stories too; but as they did not know of any cornfield where such long ears were to be found, they had to take it out in wishing; and thinking what a hundred thousand pities it was that the fairies had all gone to No Man's Land, or they would have had a fine, long pair of ears for George's use, marching to Washington, straight through Baltimore, without stopping to inquire whether they might come.

Soon after, Aunt Fanny went home. She had been very busy the latter part of the month of December, writing letters for the "Great Union Fair," which had been held in the city. All her letters were to children. I wonder if the children who got these letters, suspected who wrote them. I wonder if the little one who got this "poetry letter," tried to find Aunt Fanny out.

"You precious little darling!
   I'm very glad you've come;
How did you leave the baby,
   And all the folks at home?
Just take a look around you,
   At the pretty things you see;
Then run up to my table,
   And give a kiss to me."

Aunt Fanny could not send the promised story until the last week in January:

but when it came, there was great rejoicing; and the children settled themselves quicker than ever they did before, to hear the interesting account of

### THE ORPHAN'S HOME.

"And whoso shall receive one such little child in my name, receiveth me."—MATTHEW xviii. 5.

DARLING CHILDREN:

As I sat here thinking how to begin my story of the "Orphan's Home," our Saviour's beautiful parable of "the grain of mustard seed" came into my mind; and that you may see how well it applies to what I am about to relate, I will copy it here.

"Another parable put he forth unto them, saying:

"The kingdom of heaven is like to a grain of mustard seed, which a man took and sowed in his field:

"Which, indeed, is the least of all seeds;

but when it is grown, it is the greatest among herbs; and becometh a tree, so that the birds of the air come and lodge in the branches thereof."

Just like a grain of mustard seed did this great charity begin.

More than ten years ago, a poor man lay in a miserable bed, dying. His little children were weeping at his bedside, for their mother had gone to heaven long before; and they did not know who to look to for food and shelter, when they should be orphans.

"Oh, that I could take you with me, my poor little children!" moaned the dying father.

Just then a lady entered the room. She had accidentally heard of the man who had been ill so long, and she had come in to help him.

She spoke to him in a voice of so much kindness, that he started up, crying, "Oh, madam! I want nothing for myself! but I would get on my knees to you for my children. I cannot die peacefully, thinking of the poverty and dreadful temptations to which they will be exposed. Left alone, orphans and penniless, who is to teach them the way to heaven?"

"Take comfort, my poor friend," said the kind lady, "your children shall not suffer want."

"But will they be taught to know and love their Saviour?" he asked, looking at her with an expression of intense anxiety.

"Yes, I will see that they are religiously brought up."

"Promise me!" he said in a hoarse whisper, for the excitement had exhausted him, and he lay panting for breath.

"I promise," answered the lady solemnly.

A thankful smile flitted over the

The Little Grain of Mustard Seed.

wasted features; and looking up, he murmured, "Thank God, I die happy."

A comfortable room was hired, and the children were placed in the care of a kind and pious woman. The little orphans soon became contented and happy. You see them in the picture, playing on the floor. The good woman went out to make some purchases, which the boy just coming in has brought; a young girl is staying with the children until their kind nurse returns.

This is the grain of mustard seed. But before long, more children became inmates of this one room, and the Right Reverend Bishop Wainwright and the other good people became interested in this truly Christian work. They soon found that there was no home for destitute, outcast children, when their natural parents were taken away, who belonged to the Church by baptism. There were not enough

Orphan Asylums in this city; for numbers were brought to them, who could not get into these other institutions, because they were full. It seemed as if God himself had called upon them in behalf of these little ones. And thus it was that this institution began.

Then the good Bishop Wainwright, who is now gone home to heaven, became President; Rev. Dr. Hawks, Vice-President; and a number of excellent clergymen and gentlemen were the managers, while as many ladies were formed into a Ladies' Committee.

The grain of mustard seed had sprung up, and its leaves unfolding more and more, made it necessary to find a larger space for it to grow. So a three-story house in Hammond street was taken, and before long, twenty happy children were living there.

Oh, how hard the ladies worked in

those few first years! The money came slowly in; but they never grew fainthearted. More and more poor little orphans came to their door, begging for a home, and the living care which their own mothers, dead and gone, could never more bestow. The house was soon filled, and a more contented family of children could nowhere be found. The kind matron loved them all, and worked with the teacher night and day to make them good and happy.

The "Orphan's Home," as it was now called, continued for some years in Hammond street. Then it was removed to two houses in West Thirty-ninth street, and the ladies who had formed the committee now became the officers, with the Right Reverend Bishop Potter and a number of clergymen and gentlemen to advise them. Bishop Potter, you know, had taken the place of the late excellent Bishop Wain-

Wright; whom I esteemed and respected more than I have words to express. I wish, my darlings, you could have heard him read the parables of our Saviour; or the glorious promises contained in the gospels. Their deep and blessed meaning, coming from his lips, seemed so simple and clear, for he read them with such admirable emphasis and point. I never listened to his preaching or reading, without a thrill in my heart, and the tears often dwelling in my eyes. It was at the request of his good and lovely daughter, for whom I have a sincere and warm affection, and who was at the time treasurer of the Orphan's Home, and one of its very best and most generous friends, that I became a manager.

You would have thought that two large houses would have been room enough; but our grain of mustard seed was now a great tree, in the branches of which many more little orphan birds must have a warm nest, and be lodged and fed; and, above all, taught the Way of Life. But there was no room. The ladies who composed the Board of Managers put their wise heads together, and concluded to ask all good Christian people to help them. How could they turn away from the cry of these little desolate ones, when the Good Shepherd and His servants in the work, these kind ladies, were ready with heart and hand to watch over and protect a larger flock of these His poor little lambs?

But there was no room!

The appeal was made, and with grateful joy they saw the money flowing into the trustees' hands in loving streams. Soon enough was collected to warrant the commencing of the building, in whose wide halls and great airy rooms hundreds of motherless and fatherless children could live, and move, and play.

On the 2d of October, 1860, the corner-stone was laid. For fear you might not know exactly what laying a cornerstone means, I will tell you as well as I can.

When a large building is to be put up, the foundation is dug, and a very large square stone is placed in one of the corners, which stone has a small hollow in the top of it.

When this much has been done, everybody interested is invited to the place, and religious services are performed in the open air, the people standing reverently around.

Then the Declaration of Independence, the daily newspapers, the coins that are in circulation for money, the previous history of the institution, if it has any, and everything else that may seem proper or interesting to the occasion, is placed in the hole. The most distinguished person present takes a trowel and some mortar and closes it up. On this the wall of the building is laid.

If, in after years, it should be pulled down, it would be very interesting to take out and look over the things that have been buried so long in the corner-stone.

I was not present when our corner-stone was laid, and I never saw the ceremony; but I believe I have given you the right idea about it.

While the new Home was building, the children were well and happy in Thirty-ninth street.

We had some little ones, whose histories were very sad. There was George Floyd, whose father was mate of a vessel which must have been wrecked and lost at sea, for she went out from New York, and was never more heard from.

And there was little Dickey, who had a cruel stepmother. She ordered him to make a fire in the stove; his clothes caught the flame, and he was dreadfully burned. The bad stepmother did nothing to heal the wounds, and he was found in this state, suffering terrible pain, and brought to the Home, and tenderly nursed till he got well.

And little Mary Canard, who took care of her dying mother, though she was only six years old, whose father was killed on Captain Peak's vessel. And one dear little boy we lost. He was twelve years old, and very good and intelligent. He had that dreadful and almost always fatal illness, membranous croup:—a kind of false skin very thick and tough grows in the throat, so that it becomes impossible to breathe or swallow. The poor little fellow seemed to realize that he was going to die. He told his belief to his kind nurses, and said, "Oh, how I wish I had been confirmed! how I wish I had promised God that I would try to lead a good life and keep His commandments."

At his request Bishop Southgate, who has always been very kind to the children, was sent for. He read and prayed with him; then laying his hands softly on the dying boy's head, implored a blessing for him.

A joyful light beamed from the little fellow's eyes; his whole countenance became irradiated with happiness, and in accents of grateful delight he exclaimed, "Oh, the bishop has blessed me!" In a few hours afterward his Saviour called him, and his gentle spirit passed away from earth, to love and serve God forever in heaven.

All the rest of our children kept in excellent health, and most of them were good and obedient. The ladies worked very hard, and, with God's blessing, all things went on well.

It was in the winter of this year, 1860, that I became a manager; and, you may be sure, I soon coaxed the ladies who had been in the institution longest, to tell me what I have already written.

In the latter part of April, 1861, the grand move took place ; and on the night of the 22d, the orphans slept in two splendid great rooms called dormitories. Nice little iron bedsteads had been provided, with comfortable mattresses, sheets, blankets, and white dimity spreads ; and they looked so cosy and comfortable I should have liked to have slept there myself. The boys have the dormitory nearest Lexington avenue, and the girls the other. Opening out of each is a nice large washroom, with dear little bath tubs, wash basins, &c., just as comfortable as it can possibly be. On the same floor are the matron's and teacher's rooms, and some very large closets, where all the children's clothes are kept.

Of course, as soon as we got a little bit

settled, we determined to have a reception, and give all the friends we invited a first-rate time. We knew they would like it all the better if they could help us along when they made us this visit: so we got up a beautiful little fair and refreshment table.

Oh, how kind everybody was! If I dared I would tell you the names of all the ladies, who made all manner of pretty things, and sent in oysters, ice cream, cakes, and almost everything good to eat that was ever heard of; but these lovely Christian people prefer to do good in secret. If I were to have their names printed they might pinch my ears, and I should not like that. But I will tell you this much. I went and only just asked Rev. Dr. Dyer, of the Evangelical Knowledge Society, to give the orphan's fair some books, and he said "Yes" so quickly that I was astonished, and began to believe that there were some people in the world who were really *glad* to be asked to do a kindness for others. Then I went to the Episcopal Sunday School Union, and just asked for books there, and they, too, said "Yes," right away; and then I went to your friends the Messrs. Appleton, and they, too, said "Yes," immediately; and that night three great packages of books came up for the Orphan's Home. Did you ever hear of any thing kinder?

I believe I must tell you of *some* of the rest. There was one of our managers, a lovely young lady with beautiful brown eyes, who seemed to feel as if she never could do enough. I don't know what she did *not* give; for so many presents came in her name that there seemed to be no end to them. She even furnished the little recitation room entirely, and bought quite an apothecary shop of medicines, so that the children might have plenty when they were ill.

Then the young ladies of the "Helping Hand of St. Mark's Church" sent us a number of beautiful things. One of our managers, who had a fine conservatory, sent in a quantity of flowers, which we made into bouquets, and put into baskets, and sold for a good deal of money. We had a present of a flagstaff from Mr. Niblo, of Niblo's Garden, and one of the lady managers gave us the flag, and on the reception day it was waving over the Home. It would fill several pages to tell all the nice things that came—so I will hasten on.

We had a three days' reception in one of the great rooms, the 14th, 15th, and 16th of May. They were opened on the first day with religious services, and were all delightful. We had the carpenters to come and build tiers of seats at the lower end of the room, one above the other, reaching nearly to the ceiling; and each day the orphans marched in two and two, and were placed in the seats, to see all that was going on. Sometimes they would sing hymns for us, and other times they sang "Jim Crack Corn" and "Dixie," and other funny songs.

One day a kind lady gave them each a ten cent piece, and they came down in a great hurry to spend them immediately. We managed to have a good many things to cost only ten cents that were marked much higher, so that the dear little things should have just what they fancied.

Then a gentleman gave them each a chance, which he paid for, in a great cake; and I wish you could have heard the clapping of hands, and hurrahing, when a boy they all liked won it. Of course he gave them all a piece, and they enjoyed it tremendously. I really was afraid some of them would be ill, they had so much cake and candy.

The great fun of all to the children

was to eat philopenas with the ladies. I do believe I eat about twenty-five. Of course I never meant to catch them; but I pretended to be very much astonished when they caught me, and when I went home to my dinner I got a basket, and put in it twenty-five great rosy-cheeked apples to pay for my philopenas. I thought these were much better for them than so much candy; and when I handed them out, the children looked highly delighted.

When the fair was over, we were surprised to find how much money we had taken, and very grateful too. Some of our pretty things were left, and we put these carefully by for our winter fair; and after a little while we settled down quite comfortably in the new Home.

The summer passed quietly away; everything seemed to go on happily, although we had very hard work to collect money enough to keep us out of debt.

You see the terrible war was now raging, and all the charitable institutions were suffering, because everybody was anxious to do all they could for the soldiers.

We took three children belonging to volunteers who had no one to leave them with, and we had one poor little fellow from Fort Sumter. He was born in the fort, and soon after abandoned by his mother, who became a very wicked woman. Then his father—who was a good soldier—was sent to Florida to help fight against the Indians, and was killed: and poor little Richard was left alone in the world, with no one to take care of him but an old woman, who washed the soldiers' clothes and worked in the fort. After the wicked and dreadful attack on the handful of half-starved soldiers, who were so heroically guarding their country's flag and honor, but who were forced to surrender, the brave Major Doubleday,

Bombardment of Fort Sumter.

hearing of our Home, sent the poor little fellow on to us, and we were very glad to give him shelter, and make him as happy as we could.

Here is a picture of that sad scene. The cannonading is still going on, while they are carrying away from the ramparts two wounded men. You see in the picture, they are feeling the heart of one of them, hoping that it still beats. Do you see the brave fellow who is planting the flag? I must tell you about him. He is a Mr. Hart. When Mrs. Anderson wanted to go on to Charleston to see her husband, whose health was very delicate, Mr. Hart escorted her. He stayed in the fort, and was there during the fight. When our glorious flag was shot down, Mr. Hart seized it, nailed it to a pole, bounded up on the ramparts, and planted it again, amidst the cheers of the men. I think it was a splendid thing to have done! General Anderson has that stained, torn, but priceless flag now; and he says he is only waiting to plant it once more with his own hands over Fort Sumter. He has one dear little boy, who is named Robert after him. I think Robbie, as they call him, ought to be a proud boy; for his father will leave him what is far above untold gold—a spotlesss and honorable name.

One dear little boy died at this time, who had formerly lived in the Home. He had been a long time ill with an incurable spine disease, and it had been thought better to remove him to St. Luke's Hospital, that noble charity, where delicate, refined ladies go to live as nurses. Here he had the tenderest care; but nothing could save his life; and shortly before he died, he sent to us begging us to let him see some of his little companions, to bid them good-by, and to entreat them to be good, so that they might meet him again in heaven. It was a peaceful, happy death.

Toward November, we began to think of our winter fair, and make preparations, for we concluded to have it about Thanksgiving day. After the fair, we intended to have a festival for the children, on our anniversary evening, which would be on the 26th of December.

The fair was a very nice one. It lasted three days; and everybody that came was so kind! and seemed to feel such a tender interest in our little orphans, that I wanted to make a speech, and tell them they were all darlings, old and young. This time, as before, we made more money than we expected; and when the fair was over, some lovely lady, who would not tell her name, sent us a present of enough beautiful brown cloth to make each of our girls a warm cloak; and to render our happiness complete at this time, our treasurer got a letter, telling her and us, that more than seven hundred dollars were coming to us from the "State Fund."

I'll just tell you what we lady managers did when we heard that. We gave three cheers! and two or three (I was one) danced round the room, laughing and shouting like crazy school-girls. Don't you think I was a frisky old soul?

The children were remarkably good about this time. They knew very well, that Christmas brought presents to them, in that kind Home; they knew they would have everything but a mother's or father's warm loving kiss on that blessed holiday. But, oh, my darlings! it seems to me that a mother's kiss was worth all the rest; and that we could not give them. Cherish and love your parents, for they are the dearest earthly friends you can have.

Well, our children—as we managers always call them—had a fine Christmas dinner. Bless their little hearts! they got lots of roast turkey and pumpkin pie that day, as well as the best of us. The evening of the next day was to be the festival.

The kind ladies from Trinity Chapel had sent us a tall tree, upon which we meant to hang our presents. The important thing was, to have the presents for all; and to make sure of this, I, for one, wrote an appeal, and mustering up my courage, marched down town with it the week before to some of the newspaper offices, which is not very pleasant to do, for you have to mount to the very top story; and it is pretty inky in every direction—all except in the good editors' hearts, which were full of loving kindness, warm and glowing. I made a speech to each of these gentlemen, and was very polite, and told them all about the orphans. You can see for yourself what dear old darlings they were! for every one of them put this notice in their papers for me, and all I had to pay were two words, which were "Thank you."

Here is the notice: "Will all the mothers please to remember in these holiday times, the Orphan's Home in Forty-ninth street, near Lexington Avenue? The poor little inmates of this institution depend solely on those who love children to make Christmas a day of rejoicing to them, and thus presents of skates, balls, common jack-knives, kites, tops, marbles, and books, for boys; and dolls, tea sets, cheap work-boxes, jumping ropes, books, etc., for girls—would be eagerly and gratefully received, and each mother who feels nightly the 'little tight clasp' of her sweet little Kate or dear little Harry, will surely remember with loving pity the desolate orphans, in whose hearts, at such times of rejoicing, notwithstanding the kindest treatment, the sorrowful cry must arise, 'I have no mother—my mother is dead!' And so we beseech you, mothers, remember these orphans."

Early in the morning, after Christmas Day, the managers went to the Home to make preparations for the evening. We worked like bees, to get the great room ready. At the lower end were arranged the benches, which went up, one above the other, nearly to the ceiling, as I told you. On these the little orphans were to sit.

Exactly opposite, at the other end, we fastened the tremendous Christmas Tree, that was sent us from Trinity Chapel. Then the presents began to pour in! Dolls, drums, balls, tops, books, and all sorts of pretty things; and we mounted step ladders, and tied them to the branches of our tree. I should think there were hundreds of cornucopias—so many kind people had sent candy, and a great many bags of blue and pink tarleton filled with candy. Ah! then I found out that there were plenty of good mothers and loving hearts in the city of New York.

When we had covered the tree in every direction, we stopped, and stared at each other; and then I said, "Dear me! what shall we do with all that is left!"

"I think we shall have to spread them out on a large table," said our kind and lovely first directress, who had been with the orphans from the very beginning, when the charity was only the little grain of mustard seed; and who loved them like her own children.

Just at that moment, the matron came in and said that the congregation of the Bishop Wainwright Memorial Church in Hammond street, had sent us a large tree and some lanterns.

You may believe that we were perfectly delighted with this news; and the tree was soon hauled in. Then we had to move our tree so as to make a place for the new one; on which it was decided to fasten with the others a number of most beautiful little lanterns, with fine artistic designs painted on them, that had been brought in by the kind, good daughter of our excellent Bishop. She was one of the managers, and took the most unwearied interest in the children. She and some of her friends had made these lanterns.

So the pretty things were carefully fastened to the branches of the new tree, with tapers inside ready for lighting, and the rest of our presents were soon flourishing up there too, making such a grand show, that I thought the children, when they saw it all, would certainly go crazy with delight.

It was now quite late in the afternoon, and we were pretty tired; and after taking one last look around, to see if everything had been done, the doors were locked, and we went to our homes to dinner.

When I got back, the children were all ready, dressed as neat as new pins, and sitting on the grand, wide flight of stairs in the hall. Their eyes were sparkling, and they had hard work to sit still, knowing that there was something wonderful for them, locked up in the great room.

Some of the company we had invited, had come; and very soon after, there was quite a crowd of ladies and gentlemen, and their children, standing wherever there was room, and looking with affectionate interest at our orphans.

A small platform had been put in the middle of the hall, on which were placed a desk and chair. This was for the

Bishop; but as he could not come, the Rev. Dr. Hobart was made chairman.

We had prayers, and the children sang a beautiful hymn. Then the annual report was read, telling the company what a pleasant time we all had enjoyed in our new Institution; how well and happy the children had been, and how grateful we were to God, and the kind friends, who had given such a beautiful and comfortable home to these desolate orphans. After the report, the trustees and managers were elected for the next year; and then Dr. Weston, one of the assistant ministers of Trinity Parish, and the chaplain of our famous Seventh Regiment, made a capital address, which pleased the children very much, for it was very short as well as very good. After him came Dr. Dyer, who always looks as grave and dignified as possible; but who loves children dearly, and knows perfectly well how to tell them entertaining stories, and make them laugh, while he keeps on his grave face the whole time. He also made an excellent address.

It was not intended, this time, to be amusing, for he spoke to the children of the freezing night outside, in which many a poor little beggar might be shivering, without food or shelter, while they were in this Home, which the warm love of the ladies, through the blessing of God, had obtained for them : but that this was not all—the greatest of their blessings was, that there they were taught to know and love their Saviour, who had died for them, and him, and all the people upon earth.

Then he turned to the company present, and said it was their sacred duty to take care of helpless orphan children, and he hoped they would each make a resolution that night to *support one orphan child the coming year.*

I told his wife that he was a perfect darling for saying this; but I did not dare to say so to him. I only hope the good people made a determination to adopt his suggestions. Then the children, and all of us, sang the Doxology, and *then* the grand time came. The large sliding doors of the great room were pushed back, and the children, coming down from the stairs, were marshalled two by two, while the company looked on.

Of course the children were to go in first. It would never have done for *us* to have had the first look. Certainly not; so I said, " They are the officers to night; we must march behind."

Many a little hand grasped mine, as I stood by to let them pass, and many a bright eye was raised to mine, with a whispered " Aunt Fanny " from their smiling lips. After they were in, we marched after, in all sorts of crooked ways; and I really don't know which sparkled most, the splendid trees or the children's eyes. Yes—I think upon the whole, the eyes were the brighter; and such a quantity of delighted " Oh's " and " Only look's," I never heard before.

Oh me! it was *such* a crowd! I ought to know, for they made me one of the waiters, to carry the presents from the trees to the children; and I got squeezed flat twenty times. And then the noise! the shouts of delight and laughter, as little eager hands were stretched out to receive the gifts! It was worth at least a dollar apiece to see so much happiness; and I really think that everybody who comes to the next festival, might as well put a dollar in the little box near the front door.

Everybody in the Home got presents, and the greatest quantity of candies; and everything went off successfully. The children were to have holiday from school, that is, more play than usual between Christmas and New Year; and I am sure they had a happy time with their new toys.

Some weeks before this, I had been put on the school committee. This is composed of three of the managers, who are specially appointed to visit the school, every day if they like, see what is wanted in the way of books, &c., hear the report of the teacher about the conduct of the children, and give plenty of advice.

The very first thing I did when I became a school committee woman, was to march right into the school room, and nod and smile at as many children as I possibly could; saying to myself, "Poor little kittens, how I love them." I suppose I might as well have said it out aloud, for the children seem to read it in my face somehow; and they bobbed their heads at me, and grinned all round their mouths.

Then I went up and shook hands very politely with the teacher. She looked pretty grim; but I put on a tremendous smile, and asked if I might speak to the children.

She said, "Certainly;" and then I went among them.

"What's your name?" I said to a pleasant-looking boy.

"Jacob," he said.

"What are you learning, Jacob?"

"Catechism, ma'am; and it's so hard I can't understand a word of it; besides which, the lesson is so dreadful long! I've got to learn two whole pages."

"Well, my dear boy," I said, "I will tell you a secret. When I was a little girl, I had to learn Catechism too; and, like you, I did not understand it at all; but I *had* to learn it *perfectly;* and *now* that I have grown up, I *do* understand it. So you must have courage, and learn the words, and try to comprehend all you can, and when you are older, you will remember it, and it will be a great comfort to you."

Then I explained some of the hard words, such as "justification" and "sanctification," and left him looking happier.

But I took very good care to make a good use of the "advice" part of my duty. I told the teacher that the lesson was a great deal too long; that two questions were quite enough to learn at a time. She did not like it much, but when I *put my foot down*, the thing has to be done; and I found, on my next visit, that short lessons were the order of the day.

You would have been amused if you could have seen the children whisper and laugh at each other, because I went down with them to dinner one day; they had meat and potatoes cut up in small tin pans, and when they had all marched in, and folded their little hands, and asked a blessing, I went up to one, and said, "Please let me taste your dinner?" She gave me the spoon, and I took a bit of meat.

"Why, that is capital!" I exclaimed; "I think I must have some more!" and I asked another girl for a taste.

So the children eat their dinner, thinking it better than usual, since "Aunt Fanny," as I told them to call me, liked it. If I had been willing, they would all have given me so much dinner that I should not have known where to put it; for you must know they had plenty and to spare.

One day, the teacher said to me: "There are ten boys, madam, who behave so badly, I do not know what to do with them. They answer me impudently; they will not learn any lessons; and one of them struck me this very morning."

" Oh dear, dear ! how very sorry I am to hear this," I answered ; " will you give me their names ? "

She took a pencil out of her pocket, and wrote on a bit of paper these names; and headed them with these dreadful words: " All intolerably insolent." *

David C——e,  Theodore S——a,
Joseph S——d,  Edward R——d,
George R——s,  George B——h,
Joseph H——l,  Jacob J——s,
James P——y,  Benny L——e.

" Oh dear ! " I repeated, quite miserable to hear such a bad account, for some of these boys I had believed to be excellent children. " I will come in the school room, Miss H——, as soon as you are settled, and speak to them."

---

\* Do not be in a hurry to believe this, as I think you will find it something of a mistake.

Nearly all the managers were sewing in one of the parlors; I went in and said, "I am going to frighten ten bad boys out of their wits."

The ladies all burst out laughing. "The idea of *your* frightening a child," they said. "Won't you let us come in and see the fun?"

"You had better take your pocket handkerchiefs out if you do, for you will be more likely to cry than laugh; but I won't let you come at all. It is too serious a matter."

They laughed at me again, and pretended to believe that I meant to give the children a stick of candy apiece; but I walked into the great school room, looking very serious, and I felt very serious too, when I saw one of the boys standing in the corner for punishment. Going up to the teacher's desk, I said, "Miss H——, don't you think it would be a good plan

"I saw one of the Boys standing in the corner for punishment."

to take all the *good* children to Central Park some day?"

"Yes, madam; but I am afraid there will not be many to go."

I looked out of the corner of my eye, and saw that the poor little orphans were gazing eagerly at me; and rapping on the desk, so as to command perfect silence, I began, in a very grave tone, this speech:

"My dear children, there is one thing I want you to believe, before I say another word, and that is, that *I love you.*"

I stopped and looked round. Oh, what glances of affection came from those orphans' eyes! and one little bit of a boy, who had been made to sit on the floor close by the teacher's desk, because the boy next him had tickled him and made him laugh out loud at prayers—this little fellow put up his hand and smoothed my dress. I took his little fat fingers in mine, and went on:

"Yes, I love you dearly. I don't expect you to be perfect children, because no one is always good; but I want you to think, how kind your Father in Heaven has been to you, to place you here; instead of allowing you to wander about the streets, learning to lie and steal, and use wicked words. The least you can do, is to try—mind, I say '*try*'—to be good and obedient. You all know that many of the greatest men in this country were poor boys, with not half the advantages you have here. There is nothing to prevent any one of you boys from some day becoming the President of the United States; there is nothing to prevent you all becoming what is far higher—that is, Christian gentlemen. But for the present, what do you think, both boys and girls, about behaving so well as to deserve an excursion to Central Park?"

A tremendous cheer followed this question, and then I went on: "Well, if you are good for two weeks, you shall go. In the mean time, I wish to see ten of you boys (I won't tell their names before the rest) next Friday in the little recitation room. I shall have something particular to say to them, and I do hope they will be such very good boys from this time to then, that what I shall say will be very pleasant; and now three cheers for Central Park."

The children made a tremendous noise; for that was what they liked to do: and I went out laughing and nodding at them.

Then I got a sheet of paper, and wrote in great letters, quite an inch long, "Central Park for Good Children;" and carrying it into the school room, I pasted it in a conspicuous place, so that all disposed to be naughty might be constantly reminded of this delightful reward for good conduct; and then I said, "Good-by, girls and boys;" and they shouted back, "Good-by, Aunt Fanny," and I left them.

The next Friday, I went again to the Orphan's Home; I had prayed for my ten naughty boys every night, and I made up my mind to be very gentle and kind to them. I took a copy of the "Independent Newspaper" with me, in which was an excellent story; the very thing to read to them. It was called "New-Year's Resolutions," and was signed "I. G. O." I wish I knew the author, so that I could thank her for writing it.*

Well, the ladies laughed at me again, and begged to peep in at the door to see

---

\* I obtained permission of one of the editors of the "Independent," to insert this admirable story. Without that permission, it would have been omitted. It was written by Miss Isabella Graham Oakley, Cincinnati, Ohio. I thank her heartily.

me frighten my naughty boys; but I would not let them. I went into the pleasant little recitation room, and found them all there.

They did not look the least alarmed, but quite pleased; so I said, "Old fellows, come and shake hands with me; then you will feel that I am a friend, and I am sure you will attend to what I say."

"Yes, indeed we will," they all exclaimed; and they very nearly squeezed my hand off.

"Now," said I, "let me hear what you have to complain of, and what has tempted you to be so disobedient and disrespectful to your teacher."

Thereupon they all commenced talking at once, and made themselves out to be the most abused boys in the world. "Such long lessons! Couldn't go out and play in the wet snow! were sent to bed for nothing at all!" &c., &c.

All the time they were talking they were playing off monkey tricks upon each other. One boy would call another suddenly, with his sharp finger-nail close to his cheek. Of course, when the other turned, his cheek would come bump against the finger. Another boy, who had his hair cut very short, was favored with experiments on it by the others: each one trying to see how much he could pinch up in a thumb and finger; and once, when I got up to open the window a little, a boy on the end of the long bench tipped it, and upset all the rest on the floor.

I could not help laughing; but at last I said, "Now, boys, it's *my* turn to speak, so be quiet." Then I told them of poor children wandering in the streets that very day, without shoes or stockings, dirty, starving, taught to lie and steal, and sure, if they grew up, to do worse and worse, till they ended their days in prison, or were perhaps hung for murder. "My dear boys," I continued, "use your reason, and see how much better you are off. You are clothed, fed, and above all, taught how to lead pure lives. You know all about your Saviour, who died for you and me. We take care of you, because we love you. I love you all dearly, and you don't know what a happy and proud woman I shall be if I live a few years longer, and hear of you boys as good, perhaps great men. There is nothing to prevent it. I am sure you would rather be good than bad. I am quite certain, when you have been bad, that your conscience makes you miserable. Is it not so?"

The tears were trembling in some of the boys' eyes; and one or two answered in a loud voice, "Yes, ma'am."

"Well, I will read you this beautiful story. It will instruct you in your duty much better than I can."

They all brightened up wonderfully at the prospect of a story, and listened to it in breathless attention. Here it is.

---

### NEW-YEAR'S RESOLUTIONS.

It was New Year's evening, and the parlors, not yet lighted, were warm and quiet, when Joel Goodwill walked listlessly in and sat down in an easy chair before the grate.

"Now is a first-rate chance to think what I will do this year," said he to himself. He thought he was alone; but he had been there only a few minutes when some one spoke to him from the back parlor. It was his father.

"Why, father, you there?" said Joel. "I thought there was no one here."

"Come here, my son," said his father. Joel obeyed, and found his father sitting before the fire in the other room; he sat down on his knee.

"I have just been reviewing my past year, and laying some plans for this New Year; have you had any such thoughts, Joel?" asked his father.

"Yes, sir," replied Joel, soberly.

"You have been making good resolutions then for the future, I suppose?"

"Yes, sir; I'm going to turn over a new leaf, and do first-rate in school this year, and home too."

"Have you looked over your past year pretty closely?"

"Not so very much."

"Have you come up to the purpose of the good resolutions you made last New Year's?"

"No, sir, I expect not; I can't remember very well all I've done, or what they were."

"Seems to me you drew up a copy of resolves then, didn't you?"

"Yes, sir."

"Suppose you go and get them, and and let us look them over."

Joel said he didn't believe he could find them; he hadn't seen them for ever so long. However, he went up to his little room, and fortunately alighted upon them quite readily, in a little drawer where he kept his certificates of merit, and some other choice things.

On his way down stairs he tried to remember what there was written on the paper; but he could not recall a line. He only recollected that he was sitting at his father's secretary drawing up his "resolutions," last New Year's day, when he came suddenly behind him with a beautiful new leather satchel for him, and that he took up the paper and talked a little about it. When he reached the parlor he handed the paper to his father, remarking, "We can't see to read by the fire."

"I think we shall make it out," replied he, turning it up so that all the fire-light might reflect from it. It was written in a large, clear hand, Joel's handsomest, and was quite legible there.

"Let us see now what you meant to do last New Year."

Joel, with some secret misgivings about the proceeding, took his seat again on his father's knee, who commenced:

"*January* 1, 1861.—Resolutions for my conduct during the coming year: 'First— I shall read in the Bible and pray faithfully every day. Dr. S. told the children last Sunday that any child who persevered in this for one year would certainly become a Christian, and I am resolved to become a Christian.'"

Here his father paused. Joel was looking very gravely into the fire.

"Well, Joel, has that resolution been kept?"

"No, sir, not long."

"How long was it kept?"

"I don't know. I kept it pretty good for a while, I know; maybe till I went away to uncle's in March."

"What caused you to give it up?"

"I don't know, sir. I expect because Ben and Charley and the rest didn't care anything for their Bibles; so I gave up reading."

"Then you have not proved what Dr. S. said, have you?"

"No, sir."

"And you are no nearer being a Christian than you were last New Year's?"

"No, sir," replied Joel, feeling uncomfortable and mortified by these searching questions. His father proceeded:

"'Second: I am resolved to remember the Golden Rule in all my conduct toward my brothers and sisters.' Well, how has that fared?"

"I've kept that, part of the time, I'm sure; not always, I suppose."

"Then you don't remember having broken it?"

"No—yes, sir; I broke it to-day when I teased Ellie."

"Is that the only time you remember?"

"I broke it last Saturday when I went off with Harry's sled."

"And yesterday when you ran off and left Benny crying alone on the sidewalk, and Christmas day when you chose the best book, and—"

"Pray, don't go on, father, don't tell me any more," interrupted poor Joel, reddening more and more as his father recalled the things he had quite forgotten. "I know I can't keep that rule; I don't believe any boy keeps it."

"You know that you *have* not kept it; not that you *can* not keep it. Well, let us go on: 'Third, I am resolved to tell the whole and exact truth always.' How about this?"

Joel's conscience and memory, now pretty wide awake, began to murmur accusations on this point too. He had always scorned to tell an open, deliberate lie, and he knew he could say Yes to a question on that point. But he felt that "the whole and exact truth" was a little different, and he feared his father's memory would be better than his, so he stammered out, "I haven't told a lie this year past; you know I couldn't, father."

"But that is not all your resolution demands. Don't you ever go beyond the truth or stop short of it, in school or in play?"

"I'm afraid I do, sir," faltered Joel, deeply humbled to be called upon for this confession.

"Do you sometimes hide what you ought to confess, or tell a story so as to conceal your share of the blame and throw it on some one else? Can you remember any such cases?

"Yes, sir, I think of some things," said he, knowing well that his father was thinking of particular cases, fresh also to his own memory. Conscience and memory were becoming most uncomfortable monitors.

Here Mr. Goodwill stirred the fire till its bright blaze fell on all objects, bringing them clearly out of the twilight, and then went on, though Joel said he thought they had better not read any more. "Fourth, I am resolved not to be absent from school or late once this year, if I am well."

"I went to Uncle Joe's in the spring, you know, so of course I couldn't keep that."

"You went from choice, though."

"Yes, sir; but I did keep it up a month, I know."

His father then went more rapidly over

the remaining resolutions, simply desiring him when he came to one he was sure of having kept, to speak. These were of various degrees of importance; resolves to be first in his Latin class, to obtain a certain prize at school, to drink no tea and coffee, to give up by-words, &c. To no one of all these could Joel say Aye, excepting to the coffee and tea resolution. That, with help from his mother, he had carried out.

The reason why this exposure was particularly mortifying, was because Joel was quite proud of being considered a pretty good boy. He had seldom been so much humbled before. After a little pause his father said, kindly, seeing the boy's troubled face, "You thought you should do all these things when you wrote this, did you not?"

"Yes, sir. I felt sure of it."

"What is the reason you failed?"

"I don't know. I didn't try, I suppose."

"Yes, you did try, for you kept your promises partially."

"I tried awhile, but I didn't stick to it."

"Very true. Do you remember something Solomon says about searching for wisdom?"

"I don't remember."

"He says, he that would have wisdom must search for her as for silver, and seek her as a man seeks hid treasure. You seek wisdom when you set before you such resolutions as these. Now if a man believes there is gold in a certain place, he keeps digging and digging for weeks, till he strikes the vein. If he were *sure* it was there, I presume he would labor for it for years. But what if, when he comes to a rock, he should throw down his pick and desert the field? Has he gained anything?"

"No, sir."

"But has lost all his time and labor, and is further from fortune than ever, by the force of shiftless, unsteady habits. Now this is a case similar to yours. You are further from being generous and true and persevering, in short from possessing Christian character, than you were this time a year ago. By your carelessness and idleness, you came out of your field without a grain of gold. Besides, by making resolves and breaking them continually, you are losing all moral power and all confidence in yourself. It were better to make no promises than to be guilty of breaking so many."

Joel's convictions were fast overcoming his feelings, and the tears where starting when he asked, "What shall I do, then, if I mustn't make any more resolutions, father?"

"I do not say you must not make any

more resolutions; but before you make them, count the cost of keeping them. You must not *break* any more resolutions. One great secret of failure is, that you get discouraged because you are not perfect. Now, if you fail one day, you should not give up, but make haste to reach your old ground to-morrow. In regard to these resolutions, probably you were not sufficiently in earnest in the first place; but in the next place, you were not wise, when you first failed a little, to give up all because you could not do all. Do you understand?"

"Yes, sir; do you think it is worth while for me to try this year? I *do* want to do right!"

"Certainly I do. By your failure you have learned a lesson which will keep you both careful and humble in future. I will help you by warning, and God will help you; but you must rely chiefly on your own *strong* determination. 'The kingdom of heaven' (that is, the attainment of righteousness, such as you set before you in your New Year's resolutions) 'suffereth *violence*, and the violent take it by force.'"

Joel has commenced anew to follow one or two all-important resolutions; how he will succeed, the year, as its daily pages are written, will keep record. Let all children who have shared his failure, and they are not a few, start afresh with him to share his victory, making his first resolution, to "*hold fast* that which is good."

I. G. O.

"Ah! what a good story this is," said I, as I finished reading, "I wish you would all try to keep some of these resolutions."

"So we will," they cried.

"I don't think you will be successful

at first. I know that I should break them many times; but if you ask God to help you, you may in time be able to overcome the continual temptation to break them."

Then we had a long friendly talk together; and I saw, here and there, a beautiful trait, or noble impulse, in these poor orphan boys. They were rude to each other, but they were not mean; and I felt sure that, rightly trained, they would become, in time, good boys and good men.

"Suppose, my dear boys," I said, "I get pen, ink, and paper, and write out these resolutions, for each of you to keep a copy in your pockets; they will help to remind you. I will only ask you to *try* to keep them. Will you promise me this much?"

They all said they would try as hard as they could.

"Will you promise me to pray to God to help you?"

They promised this with downcast eyes and serious faces.

Then I said: "Well, let us see how you can mind me to begin. I am going into the committee room for the pen, ink, and paper. I expect you to sit quite still, till I come back; will you promise me this?"

"Oh yes, ma'am; we won't speak or stir from our seats," they all cried.

"*I believe you*," I said. I wish you could have seen their eyes sparkle when I said that! They were so glad that I put trust in them.

I went to the committee room, and there the first directress began to talk to me; and I staid much longer than I at first intended. When I went back with my writing materials, I listened an instant at the door. It was perfectly still.

"We have not moved or spoken," said all the boys at once.

"*I believe you*," I answered. "You are first rate fellows! not so bad, after all. I think there must have been some mistake about that bad conduct. You can behave so well when you try. I hope it is a mistake that will never happen again. I came in this room feeling very unhappy about you; but now I am very much encouraged. What do you think about being called the ten best boys in the school?"

They chuckled and grinned at this; and one boy gave another a sly poke, and said, "Here's the best boy! he hasn't known a single lesson these six weeks;" and another said, "No! this is the best boy; he broke three panes of glass last night in one of the play-room windows;" and another, "Oh, no; this is the best boy, because he's got such a big wart on his nose."

I let them talk, while I wrote on ten half pages of note paper these resolutions:

"1*st*. I will read the Bible, and pray, night and morning

"2*d*. I will try to keep the Golden Rule.

"3*d*. I will always tell the exact truth."

"There," said I, "that will do." So I gave one paper to each, with a few earnest words; and shook hands with them again, as they promised me to try to keep them; and then they went softly back into the great school-room.

I looked in a few moments after, and saw that they were quietly studying.

The next Friday, I had my ten naughty boys in the little room again.

"Well," said I, "how did you keep the resolutions?"

"Oh!" cried Jacob, "I've broken the Golden Rule."

"Why, how?" I asked.

"Why, ma'am, David had a ball, and he lent it to me, and when he wanted it again,

I would not give it to him, but threw it as far as I could out of the window."

"Oh, Jacob!" I exclaimed, "how well you understood what the rule is! Tell me; what *ought* you to have done?"

"I ought to have given David his ball when he asked for it."

"Why?"

"Because, ma'am, I would have liked him to do so to me."

"Ah, yes; that is it. You understand, and you have sinned wilfully. I am very sorry, dear Jacob; but it is never too late to mend; and I am glad you have had the honesty to confess what you have done; that is a noble trait in you Jacob, and I want you to come and kiss me."

The boy burst out crying at this; and as he kissed my cheek with his trembling lips, I said to myself, "*This* a bad boy? No, he is a splendid boy!"

Don't you see that my making him

feel that I *loved* him, was the way to his heart? I think if ladies would be just as tender to poor children as they are to their own, it would have a wonderful effect. Only make a child feel that you love him, that he is more than a poor little beggar dependent upon your charity, and he will try to deserve all your kindness.

All the boys had to confess they had broken their resolutions; and to all I talked kindly; but one of them whispered to another: "She did not give us any kiss." Fortunately I heard this, and I said, "Boys, I am going to give you another chance. I shall bring a beautiful little book next time, and the boy who has behaved the best, shall have the book. I shall not ask the teacher. I shall depend entirely on your own accounts of yourselves, for I intend to trust you, and believe what you say. To make myself certain that you would scorn to deceive me, and above all, that you would not offend Our Heavenly Father by a falsehood, I wish you all to shake hands once more, and give me a kiss; then I am certain you will mean to keep at least the third resolution. What is it?"

"I will always tell the exact truth," they shouted.

So they kissed my cheek, and then I read to them a story I had written some time before for that dear little magazine, "The Standard Bearer." Here is the story, and the good minister's name is Dr. Prime.

### THE MINISTER'S STORY.

The other day Aunt Fanny was talking with a good minister, and asked him which he thought were best for children—funny stories or serious ones.

"Well," said he, "suppose I relate

what happened to me last week, and leave you to guess?"

"Oh! that will be delightful!" I answered. "I am just as fond as the children are of hearing stories, and, as they say: 'Please begin right away.'"

"Very well. Last week I was in Rochester, in this State. There is a very large orphan asylum there, and I was invited to visit it, and address the boys. I was very glad to do so; and when I entered the chapel, I found several hundred boys waiting for me—some with bright, honest faces, some looking full of mischief and fun, and all wondering what the minister was going to say, and no doubt hoping he was a good kind of a minister, who did not think it wrong to play.

"I fancy they must have seen something that pleased them in my face; for when I said, 'Boys, which would you rather have, a story or a sermon?' they all shouted out merrily, 'A story! a story!' and some added: 'Let it begin, "Once upon a time," for that is the best kind of story.'

"Very well, boys, you shall have a story, and it shall begin just as you say.

"Once upon a time, a little girl was playing in a garden, rolling hoop, jumping rope, and talking to her doll. After a while, she ran to her mother, who was sitting upon a bench that was under a wide-spreading tree, and asked if she might have some luncheon. Her mother went into the house, and soon returned with a small basket, and gave it to the little one. What was her surprise and delight, when she peeped in, to find a light, delicate biscuit, a nice cake, a beautiful ripe peach, and a little cherry tart.

"Lucy (for that was her name) placed all these things on the bench, and clapping her hands with delight, exclaimed: 'Oh! how nice they all look! What a fine party dolly and I will have with them!' Then she put the biscuit in dolly's white kid hand, who smiled sweetly all the time, and taking the cake in her own, began to eat it.

"Just then a poor woman approached the gate. Holding fast to her ragged dress was a little boy, so wan, so thin, so starved-looking, that Lucy stopped eating, and gazed pityingly at him.

"'*Oh! what nice white bread!*' said the poor boy.

"'It is *not* bread—it is cake,' said Lucy.

"'Alas! little lady,' said the poor woman, 'he does not know what cake is; he is too glad to get a crust of bread.'

"'Poor boy!' said Lucy kindly. 'How strange not to know what cake is! Here, take it.'

"He seized the cake, and in a moment he had eaten it up.

"Then Lucy took up the cherry tart, and stretching out her hand, said, in her sweet voice: 'Eat this too, poor boy!'

"He did not need to be asked twice; and the tart soon disappeared.

"'Now, take this,' said Lucy, handing him the beautiful peach.

"With joyful eagerness the boy swallowed the peach, while the generous child looked on, her face glowing with delight; and then she took the biscuit out of dolly's hand, and gave it to the poor little fellow, who finished it in double quick time, and dolly smiled just as sweetly as ever, when she gave up her biscuit, which was very good-natured in her, under the circumstances. Then the poor woman poured out thanks and blessings upon the head of the dear little girl, and upon her mother who had given the poor woman a piece of money; and she and her son went on their way with grateful hearts, the little boy looking back at Lucy as long as he could see her.

"Then the mother took the little girl in her arms, and kissed her, and said: 'My darling! you have not had any luncheon.'

"'Oh, mamma!' said Lucy, her face still glowing with pleasure, '*I feel as if I had eaten it all myself.*'

"You see, boys, that the noble-hearted little child was even more happy in giving than the poor boy was in receiving; and I want you every day of your lives to love one another, and be generous and kind one to another—to do as you would wish to be done by, for this is what little Lucy did.

"God has laid His hand of blessing on your heads; He has placed you who have no earthly parents in this pleasant home, to show you that He is your Father; and the only way in which you can prove your gratitude to Him is, to 'Love one another;' and if you love one another, you will keep

His commandments. Love your teachers, and you will obey them. Love God, and you will keep His commandments.

"And now, which do you think you have had—a sermon or a story?

"'A story!' shouted some of the boys.

"'A sermon!' shouted others.

"'BOTH!' shouted still more."

Dear little readers, which do you think it was—a story, a sermon, or BOTH?

I asked my boys when I finished whether they thought it was a story or a sermon, and they shouted just like the other boys; some, that it was one, and some the other; but they liked it very much, and thanked me for reading it. "Then I said, I will give this little 'Standard Bearer' to any one of you: which one shall it be?"

"Give it to Jacob," shouted nearly all the boys, for they all liked him.

I handed it to Jacob; and what do you think he did? He gave it to the smallest boy, saying, "*I* think little Joseph ought to have it."

That was really noble, because he was very fond of reading, and I knew that he wanted it; but the little fellow looked so wishful, that Jacob *did as he would wish to be done by*, and the bright glow on his face showed how happy this little sacrifice had made him.

And I!—wasn't I happy? Yes, indeed! And I bade them all good-by, and promised to bring a "real nice book" next time, and went back to the room where the ladies were sewing, with such a joyous expression on *my* face, that they asked if my ten bad boys had all flown away to the moon? to which I gravely answered: "The *badness* has flown away, and left ten splendid boys."

The next Friday came; and, true to my promise, I carried a book which contained a very interesting story of two children who lived in Gibraltar with their father, who was an officer in the English army. It described the battles the English fought on sea and land to obtain possession of that famous rock; a trip the children took to Africa, which you know is just opposite; and was so full of information about the customs and manners of the people who lived there, that it made a delightful little history, told in the form of a story.

My ten boys met me in the little room with joyful greetings; but I am sorry to say they had to confess that they had not kept the resolutions any better than before. Still, as they showed plainly that they wanted to be good, I was puzzled to whom to give the book, as they all seemed to have behaved equally naughty as well as good.

"I don't want to take the book

home again," I said; "whom shall I give it to?"

"Give it to me!" "Give it to me!" "No, to me!" each one shouted.

I looked reproachfully at them, and said quietly, "Then it seems you are all selfish."

At this they began to call out, "Give it to Jacob," "Give it to Theodore," &c.

"Well," I said, "you have all been bad alike, according to your own confessions. I will draw lots for you, on condition that the boy who gets the book shall lend it cheerfully to the rest in turn to read, and the rest of the boys must feel willing and happy to have the winner keep it. Will you try to do this?"

They eagerly promised. So I cut ten little squares of paper, while they gathered round me and looked on with the greatest interest, and on each bit of paper I put a boy's name.

"Now, boys, you will all have a chance.

See—I will roll up each bit, and tumble them all together in this saucer; and then who shall take them out one by one?"

"All of us," they cried.

"No, that won't do. Let Joseph, as he is the smallest boy; and mind, the *last* one wins."

"Yes, ma'am," they said; and now it was funny to see the intense importance with which little Joseph put in his thumb and finger among the papers. He took one, dropped it, and took another and handed it to me.

You could have heard a pin drop while I unfolded it; and when I read "Joseph," the little fellow's face grew so long that I felt very sorry, and wished I had bought ten books.

"Never mind, my little fellow, you will read it, you know," I said; "and you will be glad for the boy who gets it—won't you?"

He brightened up in a moment, and drew another and another till only two were left.

The two boys whose names had not yet been called were now the objects of the highest interest to the rest, and they were laughing and telling Joseph to stir the bits of paper up well. He drew again—"James" was the name—and the book belonged to Theodore, whose bright black eyes danced with delight, for his was the name left in the saucer.

"But I will let you all read it," he said, "even before I do—and little Joseph first."

I was delighted to hear him say this, and still more delighted that not a mean expression or covetous look was to be seen in the faces of my good boys. They stood the hard test nobly, and that day I was very happy.

Soon after this my daughter was taken

very ill, as you know, and I could not go for many weeks to the Home: when I did go, I found everything pleasant and quiet, but the boys were restless and troublesome. So I made a report at the beginning of the next month, stating that they did not have enough to do. You see our girls learn to sew, wash and iron, and keep house. But we were puzzled to find suitable work for our boys; and I proposed in my report that they should learn some mechanical trade, and recommended that the managers should begin with shoemaking.

To my great gratification, the ladies all approved of this; and I can tell you I soon hunted up a shoemaker who was willing to come and teach them for a little money, and in a week there was a dozen boys provided with tools, leather, &c., hard at work, and very happy learning to make and mend shoes.

Such piles of shoes as wanted mending, so many little toes had rubbed out holes, that I had to laugh, for they all looked as if *they* were laughing with their mouths wide open. I told the boys, that as soon as they knew how to make shoes well, they must make a pair of boots for *me*, for which I would pay them just as much as I did my shoemaker in Broadway. They were delighted at this, and ran their tongues out, and sewed away, and promised to try their very best.

About this time we got a new teacher, a kind, grave man, whom the children liked very much. I wanted to see exactly how he managed with the children; so one day I went into the school room, and asked to have my boys read for me. The teacher gave them each a history of the United States, and handed one to me. Every boy read a paragraph in turn, and I was surprised at their improvement. They minded their stops, and generally placed the emphasis properly.

While they were reading, one little bit of a girl after another crept up to me and leaned confidingly against me; and before the reading was through, I had five of these motherless little ones nestling close to my knees. You see they did not have to sit very quiet, or learn much, because they were none of them five years old; and if they did not make a noise, they could move about a little. I said to one of them, "Well, little Kate, did you get a doll last Christmas?"

"Yes, ma'am," she answered; "and I broke it all to pieces."

Then she gave a little chuckling laugh, and looked so roguish, that I pinched her fat red cheeks. If you go to the Orphan's Home, ask to see Kate, and Lillie, and Maggie; for they are three nice little girls. Just before my daughter got so well that

## 94 THE ORPHAN'S HOME MITTENS.

I could return to my pleasant work at the Home, something happened which filled me with grief. Our kind first directress, and my dear friend the treasurer, resigned their offices. They grieved about it even more than I did. They had been with the orphans so long, and had worked so hard for these poor children.

But it could not be helped. They thought it best for others to take their places, although they would remain just as warm friends as ever to the little ones.

✻ ✻ ✻ ✻ ✻ ✻

And now I believe I have written all that there is to relate about my children in the Home, up to this time. If you feel an interest in them, and you and I live another year, at the end of it I will tell you all that happens during the year. Would you like it?

That was the end. The children clapped their hands and said, "Oh, mamma! this is the very best story yet. Dear little orphans! how sorry we are they have no mothers and fathers! What *should* we do if you should die!"

At this distressing thought, they rushed to their mother, and clasped her with I don't know how many arms, and kissed her forehead, and eyes, and nose, and chin, and the back of her head, till from very nearly crying they all got laughing; and two or three tumbled down in a heap together on the carpet. "Oh, dear, dear!" cried the little mother, laughing and struggling, "you will kill me if you love me so desperately; I shan't have half a nose or quarter of an ear left between you all. Shoo! Boo! Bang!"

They all fell off laughing, pretending to be shot; and soon after, with thanks to Aunt Fanny and their kind mother, the children went to bed.

## "THE BATTLE OF ROANOKE ISLAND."

THE reading of the account of the "Orphan's Home," had taken several evenings; during which the mittens had greatly increased. For some time after this, there had been no story. The little mother, though she tried to keep it to herself, was in great anxiety about her soldier son, who had gone down with General Burnside's brigade to North Carolina. She had read the general's address to his men, in which he appealed to their honor and humanity, and asked them to treat the property of the enemy with unfailing protection and respect; and wounded soldiers who might fall into their hands, with the utmost kindness and attention; ending in his conviction that they would be as noble hearted as he knew they were brave. "Ah," she thought, "this looks as if a battle was intended."

Then the stirring news came of the capture of Roanoke Island, with a few words about the bravery of the men and the terrible hardships they had endured, fighting through dense swamps and almost impenetrable thickets.

Oh! how terrible were the next few days passed in woful, trembling suspense. There was no official report as yet, of the killed and wounded; and the hours of many a household like those of the little mother's, were passed in alternate prayers, hopes, and fears.

On the afternoon of the 14th February, Harry and Johnny went out together. They felt so distressed about their beloved brother, they could not sit still in the house. Near Union Park they met Gus Averill, one of Harry's friends, and some other lads. Of course the boys immediately began talking of the battle of Roanoke Island; as Gus had an elder brother in the same company with George.

"Oh, Harry!" cried Gus, "have you had any news from your brother? Is he safe?"

"We don't know yet," answered Harry sorrowfully. "Have you heard from your brother Walter?"

"No. My mother is almost crazy. That dear Miss Wilmer, to whom he is engaged to be married, comes and tries to comfort mother; but it always ends in her laying her head on mother's breast and crying, oh! so pitifully! and then mother cries; and that breaks my heart."

His lips quivered as he spoke, and the lad standing by him threw his arms affectionately over his neck, while Harry and Johnny looked grieved enough.

Near Union Park they met Gus Averill and some other Lads.

"Oh, if this dreadful war could only be ended!" cried a bright-looking boy, clenching his stick, and striking it on the pavement. "Why don't the President just proclaim freedom to every soul at once! My father says that would end the trouble double quick!"

"If the President thought so," said Harry, "he would soon say the word. I think he is the very best President we ever had; so honest and *straight out.* He don't think of himself; only of his country, and what is best for her. He's a dear, good old fellow, and if I saw him, I should just go up to him and say, 'I love you, President Lincoln, for you are an honest man.'"

"And so should I," said Johnny. "Aunt Fanny declares that anybody else's head would have become addled and utterly confounded by this time, with all this terrible war and confusion; but Mr.

Lincoln's HONESTY OF HEART keeps his *head* clear, and so he does his duty; while his enemies snap and snarl; but they *never* 'catch a gudgeon.' Do you know Aunt Fanny?" he asked.

"Oh yes," cried all the boys.

"Well, her daughter wrote such a nice piece about the President, that I have learned it. If you like, I will tell it to you."

"That we should!" cried the boys; so Johnny in a clear voice began:

"Fling out the broad banner! make ready each hand!
  For the cry of Disunion is rife in our land;
  Each day may behold a new battle begun,
  And true blood must flow ere the victory's won.
  Then loud let the message ring out to the South:
'Republicans have but one heart and one mouth.
  For the freedom we love, for the land we adore,
  *For the Union*, and Abraham Lincoln—hurrah!'

"What! brothers and countrymen! mean you to part,
  With a curse on each lip, and revenge in each heart?

What! fly from a government simple, but grand,
Your future to build on foundations of sand?
No! Stop, while 'tis time, oh ye men of the South,
Let us have for our country one heart and one mouth,
And, brothers once more in the land we adore,
We'll shout 'For *The Union Forever!* Hurrah!'

"Then let enemies thicken; we'll never despair,
Where unity is—behold victory there!
Disunite—in the ruins of home you will lie,
*In* Union you conquer—without it, you die.
Oh then, let it come from the North and the South:
'We have but one country, one heart, and one mouth.
For the freedom we love, for the land we adore,
FOR THE UNION, and ABRAHAM LINCOLN—Hurrah!'"

By the time Johnny had finished, a dozen more lads and some gentlemen had gathered round to listen. The little fellow's color mounted high, but he went on with admirable emphasis and animation to the end; and then let me tell you that, when he uttered the last "Hurrah," the boys snatched their hats off, and joined in with such a *will*, that the stunted old trees in the Park cracked again! and if it was not a very immense mass meeting, it was a highly respectable one, and perfectly unanimous.

"That was splendid!" said the bright boy, who had advised the President to proclaim universal freedom. "I love Aunt Fanny's daughter for writing it; and you may tell her so. I wonder if she wrote the beautiful little poem mother read to me the other day from the Rebellion Record. It set her crying; and I had hard work, I can tell you, to keep my face from puckering up."

"Oh, can you remember it?" asked some of the boys. "Do try."

"Yes; I learned it, only reading it twice after mother had read it to me. I don't know as you will like it as much as I did; but I've got a little brother, who says just such things the whole time."

"Why, so have we," cried Johnny, "lots of them! so come let's hear it."

The little fellow put his finger on his lip, to think for a moment, and then began in a low voice; all the boys crowding round so as not to lose a word.

"Willie stood at the window—
　Little Willie, five years old—
Watching the rainbow colors,
　Fading in sunset's gold,
Red pennants, and streamers of fire,
　On the blue expanse unfurl;
And over the red the white clouds lie,
　Like floating mists of pearl.

"'Isn't it beautiful, mamma?'
　And the dark eyes grow so bright,
They almost seem to catch the gold
　Of the sky's wild glory light.
'See! There is the red, mamma,
　And there is the beautiful blue;
Did God make the blue and red?
　Did He make the white clouds too?

"'And away up in the sky,
   Oh! see the little bright star!
Why! *God is for the Union?*
   Isn't He, mamma?'"

"What a dear little fellow he was," cried Johnny. "Yes, God *is* for the Union. Why can't everybody see it?"

"All in good time—His good time," said his brother; "come, Johnny, let's us go back to mother." And so they separated; and our boys, Harry and Johnny, walked quickly home.

They had not been in the house ten minutes, when the postman's peculiarly loud and impatient ring was heard. The little mother's heart stopped beating for a moment, while the children, too anxious to wait for a servant to come, rushed in a body to open the door. One united scream of joy greeted the dear brother's well-known handwriting.

"Safe! safe!" they cried, as they ran

with the precious letter to their mother, who had turned so ghastly white that she seemed to be dying. It was a thick enclosure. With trembling, eager fingers, the envelope was torn away. Within was a long letter written on several sheets of paper, which were closely wrapped around a miniature of a beautiful young girl; a short, thick lock of dark curling hair, and a small card, on which was a tiny but most exquisite painting.

It represented a dark and stormy sea; the angry waves beating furiously against a great rock, which stood like a tower of strength in the midst of the waters.

On the rock far above, a cross, steadfast and immovable, was planted, from which all the light in the picture came.

The inscription below was: "Our faith;" and on the back was written, "For dear Walter's birthday."

"These must belong to some one else,"

said the little mother in a low, sobbing voice. Then looking again at the miniature, she uttered a cry of grief, as she saw that it was a likeness of one she knew and loved dearly. She took up the letter, and read, half blinded with tears—

"*February* 12*th*, 1862.

"Darling Mother, Father, Brothers, and Sisters:—I have had my wish. I have been in a battle and, I hope, did my duty. I have come out unharmed; and I thank God humbly, for his goodness and mercy.

"We went through the inlet on the sternwheel boat 'Cadet,' February 7th. Soon General Burnside directed Lieutenant Andrews to take a boat's crew and ten soldiers, and pull for the shore to take soundings and examine the landing.

"Lieutenant Andrews, who is a cool, brave fellow, went through this enterprise splendidly. I had the good fortune to go with him. He took the soundings, went ashore, saw the glitter of bayonets, and was convinced that the landing was commanded by the rebels.

"Just as he returned to the boat, a number of men sprang up like lightning from the tall grass, and fired at us. One bullet took effect; one poor fellow was severely wounded.

"Then our vessels bombarded them. A hurricane of shot and shell was poured into their battery, till they seemed to be enveloped in one sheet of white smoke and flame; for we had set their quarters on fire. But with a desperation that filled me with a sorrowful admiration, they still worked at their guns.

"Then the rebel gunboats came down upon our vessels, and the brazen throats of our guns opened upon them with such deadly effect, that a boat of the enemy's was soon enveloped in flames. One of those awful hundred-pound shells from a Parrott gun fell and exploded on her deck.

"At four o'clock in the afternoon, our general made a circuit of the fleet. A shell from the enemy was aimed at his boat, but it exploded, fell into the water, hurting no one. The fighting continued till six o'clock, when our vessels hauled off, and all became quiet. No light was seen on shore but the red glow of the burning ruins of the enemy's quarters. They had fought bravely; and though in the wrong, I could not help feeling a respect for their courage, while I condemned their cause.

"The landing of our brave fellows was effected in a wonderfully short time; for we had no trouble from the enemy, as the men who fired on Lieutenant Andrews and his crew, were sent scampering into the woods by a shell from one of our boats, which went howling like a fiend through the air, and fell down upon them.

"But it began to rain, and in a cold driving storm we waded through the swamp, the rank grass up to our eyes, until we came out on a sandy plain. We tore up a rail fence, and at eleven o'clock that night our bivouac fires spangled the earth.

"You may imagine how much rest we got, with nothing but our thin overcoats to protect us. But our courage flamed up bright in spite of the weather; and when the order to form was given next morning, we rushed to our places with hearty good-will.

"Generals Foster and Burnside came up and said a few pleasant words. Then the reconnoissance was made, and we soon heard firing. We were ordered to advance. The men laughed and joked with each other as they marched, while our great guns boomed and thundered, and the fierce, incessant shriek of rifle shot filled the air.

"We went a mile, then two, and now the shot rattled among the leaves, and men came past carrying the brave Massachusetts boys, pierced by ball and bayonet, showing frightful bleeding wounds. As they were borne to the rear, they would pass us with a smile on their ghastly faces; or would utter a faint, trembling cheer, and the words, 'Never give up, boys, Victory or death!' and then a grand heroic fire would blaze up in their eyes.

"On we marched, till we heard cheers and screams of fury mingling with the thundering of the guns. Thick smoke, through which came flashes with a gleam like tiger's eyes, enveloped us, and the whistle of the bullets rushed close past our ears.

"We were under fire; and now, dear

mother, I breathed a prayer to God to nerve my arm and heart. Not a weak soul—not a coward was in our ranks. I looked around, and saw in every resolute face a look which plainly said, 'Glory, or a grave.'

"Then our colonel gave the order to fire. Directly in front of us was the famous redoubt, of which we had heard so much; and we could see riflemen in the trees, under the turfed walls, and behind every possible cover. But we obeyed the order with a *will*, and for an hour we fought. Not a soul flinched. As the balls struck our men, and they fell, they were carried to the rear, and the ranks closed up without wavering. I seemed turned into stone; my heart hardened. I saw a ball strike poor Walter Averill, who fought at my side. He gave a low cry, and sank to the ground. Two privates carried him to an ambulance, and I turned away with my heart of granite harder, stonier than ever. It seemed impossible to feel sorrow. Suddenly a wild cheer rose up above the awful din. *Our flag waved from the redoubt!* Another! another! The battle was won!

"Roanoke Island was ours! with all the enemy's guns, and three thousand men with their arms, ammunition, and stores. The victory was complete.

"There was one young fellow, dear mother, who deserved to be made a general. Oh, mother! he was only seventeen years old—three years younger than I. He was ordered to plant a battery of six twelve-pounder boat howitzers from the vessels in the advance of the centre. He dragged these through the swamp and placed them in position. They soon began to thunder and flash into the enemy, who returned the fire with such fury and desperation that every man, one after the

The Battle of Roanoke Island.

other, was shot down, and he was left alone. The chaplain of the Twenty-fifth Massachusetts, Rev. Mr. James, then rushed up and worked at one of the howitzers till his ammunition gave out, and he had to retire. Still this undaunted boy kept on loading and discharging his gun, now entirely alone, and a mark for the most terrible galling fire; and he did this until the enemy had surrendered.

"What a heroic soul lives in that brave boy's body! You may be sure that I found him out when the battle was over, and I just took him in my arms and hugged him tight. I hope we shall be fast friends as long as we live. His name is Benjamin H. Porter, and he lives in New York State. So give three cheers for him, and our grand old State."

The children, though in tears at hearing of all their brother had passed through, complied with his wish, and heartily cheered the brave young midshipman and the dear old State. Then the little mother went on reading—

"The grand, comfortable wooden camps of the enemy were of course turned over to our use; and our miserable captives, who certainly *looked* like mudsills—though we have the *name*—were bivouacked outside, well guarded.

"When the madness—for such hardness must have been a temporary frenzy—left me after the battle was over, I got permission to hunt up poor Walter Averill. I soon found him, lying in a room, with five other wounded men. His eye caught mine—a thankful gleam came into them as he beckoned me to him.

"'Oh, Walter!' I cried, my heart now softened and beating loud with sorrow, 'we've gained the victory, but you lie here wounded'—I stopped, for my voice became choked.

"'Yes, George, and dying,' he hoarsely whispered. 'Thank God you have come. I shall never see my home again. Look here.'

"He raised his bloody shirt, and I saw the life-blood slowly ebbing away, from a ghastly wound in his breast.

"Oh, mother, don't think me weak; but I burst into tears, crying, 'Walter, Walter, what *will* your mother do?'

"'Will you take a message to her and all the dear ones at home?' he answered. 'Tell them I fought bravely, and they must not grieve, for victory spread her pinions over my bloody bed, and took away the sting of death. Tell brother Gus he must comfort mother, and stand with his arms clasped lovingly round her, when the troops come marching home without me. Tell him to look upon them with proud, steadfast eyes; for his brother filled his own place with honor in the ranks, while he was among them, and did not fear to die. It is God's will. He knows best.'

"'And, George, there is another. She who was to have been my dear wife when I came back.' He turned away his head, and through my own blinding tears I saw the great woful drops roll down his cheeks.

"'Oh, Walter,' I sobbed, 'it's too hard!'

"'Next Tuesday would have been my birthday,' he said. 'I should have been twenty-two years old. Some little precious gift will be sure to come from Helen. If it comes in time, will you lay it on my breast to be buried with me? But if too late, take care of it, and return it to her when you find an opportunity. And cut one or two locks of my hair for my mother, and my poor—' his face changed all at once. With a last, dying effort he put his hand to his neck and drew out a ribbon, to which was attached a miniature, and placed it in my hand. Then in a voice faint, hoarse, dying, he murmured 'Mother— Helen.' One fluttering sigh, and he lay quite still. He was dead.

"The first pale moonbeam came creeping in, and rested softly on his face. It was calmly looking down on the red sand of the battle field with its bloody corses strewn here and there; and it was shining as calmly upon you at home, dear mother, who knew nothing then of that dreadful scene. As I thought of this, and the anguish the events of that day would make for Walter's family, and many another beside, I threw my head down on my dear lost comrade's bed, and sobbed till I thought my heart would break.

"I send the miniature, the locks of

hair, and the little package that came the day after we buried him, with this letter. You will have to make these sad tidings known to his family. No one can do it as tenderly—but, 'Walter *killed!*' There is no softening of that terrible word.

"Good-by, dear mother, and all my dear ones. Write often to me; and, above all, pray for

"Your loving son and brother,

"GEORGE."

As the letter concluded, Harry, who loved his friend, Gus Averill, next to his own brothers, exclaimed, "Oh, poor Gus!" —threw his arms on the table, and laying his forehead on them, gave way to such terrible convulsive sobs that it seemed as if his very heart was bursting with grief. The poor children could not comfort him, for they were crying themselves. Grateful that their own dear brother was safe, they could still feel the sharp sting of sympathetic sorrow at their friend's loss. No family had taken a greater interest in the children's evening work for the soldiers than Mrs. Averill's; and for the first time that winter, the whole evening was passed by them alone, and in a mournful silence; for the little mother went immediately on her sad and terrible errand, and did not return till quite late.

But a loving, thankful letter was to be despatched without delay to the dear son and brother; and as there was a prospect of his remaining some time in his present quarters, a box of comforts was eagerly prepared.

Every one of the children wrote letters perfectly running over with love and joy at his safety; and Willie and Bennie, with immense efforts and a great deal of rubbing out to make them better, sent to him divers pictures which they had drawn on purpose to please him.

Bennie sent this—which he called General Floyd—with a shield with a C in the middle for "Confederate," and four legs to show how very fast he could run. I am sure we all ought to be glad he *did* run; for the expression of his face, if Bennie's portrait is correct, is enough to strike terror and dismay to the heart of every loyal soul.

Willie made a likeness of President Davis, with a crown on his head, and pointing with a grin to the stars, which represented the Southern States.

Then Bennie made an elegant picture of the army of the Potomac, with the American eagle in one of the corners looking approvingly at it, all travelling down together to kill a turkey buzzard and a mud turtle, which somebody told him were Southern productions. He put

Beunie's Portrait of Genl. Floyd.

THE NEW YORK
PUBLIC LIBRARY

ASTOR, LENOX AND
TILDEN FOUNDATIONS
R          L

Willie's "Cavalry Picture."

numbers on the heads of those he meant for our generals, also on the guns, and Southern celebrities; and left the American eagle and the privates to get along as well as they could without them.

When Willie was favored with a glance at this remarkable picture, he concluded that it would never do for him to take no notice of the army; so he devoted himself to the production of a cavalry scene. Here it is. I think the horse with five tails and a square lump on his back, is particularly fine, or funny; but Willie is very proud of the whole thing, and wants to have it framed, and hung up in the parlor when George comes home.

A few days after, George wrote another letter, which was much more cheerful. He said:

"*February 17th*, 1862.

" DEAR MOTHER:

" We are quietly bivouacked here, and

everything is coming right except the loss of our friends.

"I send you a rough sketch of the tent in which we worshipped on Sundays. We have the Presbyterian form of service, and every one seems to enjoy the holy quiet of the day. It seems so dreadful that most of our battles have been fought on Sunday. Ah! I am called. I will write more to-morrow if I can.

"*February* 23d. I am so glad that my letter did not go the other day, as it gives me the opportunity to thank you all—dear, dear ones! for your letters. The box, of course, of which you speak, cannot be here near as quickly, as the express has thousands upon thousands to deliver.

"But Bennie and Willie! what shall I say to express my delight at their elegant pictures! I have pinned them to my tent, and I look at them and think that never were such funny, darling little

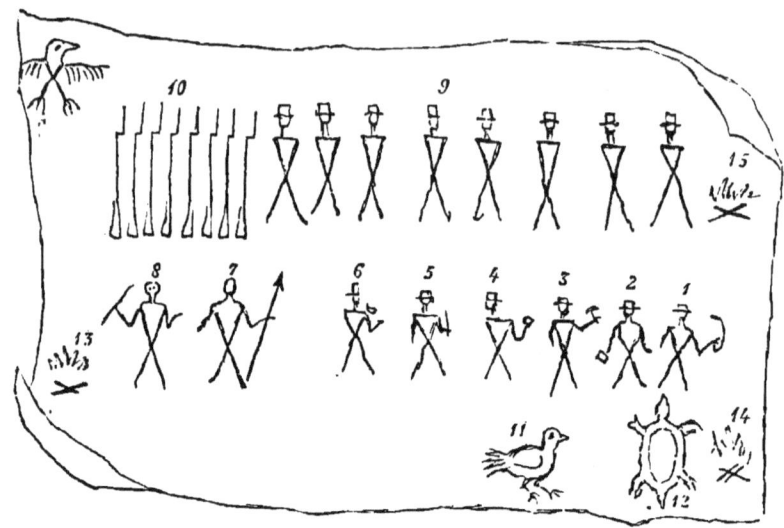

The Army of the Potomac.

THE NEW YORK
PUBLIC LIBRARY

ASTOR, LENOX AND
TILDEN FOUNDATIONS
R             L

brothers before! and certainly never were more perfect pictures of the kind. Here is a drawing of an ambulance, which I

send in return: two poor wounded soldiers are inside, and two sitting behind with their arms in slings; and here is one I have made of the celebration we had yesterday in honor of Washington's birthday. It was a pretty rough affair; and the few *natives* who gathered round, did not remind me in the least of New York. The country people here are very uncouth and ignorant; and do not seem to know what comfort is, as we understand it. They " reckon " about everything; and when they consider themselves fortunate in any possession, they say they "reckon" they have a "pretty smart chance" of it.

"I am cheerful during the day, but in my dreams at night, I still hear the deadly whiz of bullets, and feel the horrible breath of the great balls and shells on my cheek. You can form no idea of the peculiar sensation it causes. Then poor Walter's dying form and words rise up in my brain; and I go over that woful scene, again and again. It will be many a long month before I can think of him without grief. He was beloved by everybody in the regiment. Tell this, dear mother, to his family.

"Tell Bennie, I think General Floyd must have used all his four legs when he ran away so fast from Fort Donelson; while that brave Commodore Foote stuck like wax to his duty, and did not leave the fort till he had put not only his own foot in it, but the foot of every man who

Celebration of Washington's Birthday.

THE NEW YORK
PUBLIC LIBRARY

ASTOR, LENOX AND
TILDEN FOUNDATIONS
R        L

helped him to take it. That's the kind of Foote for us! Isn't it, Bennie?

"And tell Willie, I showed his picture of Jeff. Davis grinning at his stars, to a darkey, who waits upon me; and he stooped over, put his hands on his knees, and said, laughing, "Hech! hech! y-a-h! Mas' Jeff. Davis, he grin toder side he mouf, bimeby; he mighty fas' wid he larf. Let ole Mas' Linkum 'lone. He knows. He make me for free, de Lord bress him!"

"Oh! oh! how I wish I could be with you all for just one day. I think I should kiss and hug you nearly to death.

"Don't forget to read my letters to Aunt Fanny, dear little old soul! I am afraid she will forget me, or will not have me hanging round her any more, now that I have got so big and clumsy. But she need not try to get rid of me. I'm a deal the strongest, and if she says she won't have me for one of her children forever and a day, I'll come home and pack her up in my cartridge box, and keep her there till she repents of her cruelty. Tell her that I would rather she should

>Stab me through,
>And shoot me too,
>And kill me, which is worse, worse, worse,

than to refuse to consider me as one of her boys.

"And now, dear sisters and brothers, I must get ready for parade. I love you all, oh, how dearly! God grant we may meet again. Pray that this awful war between brothers, which is literally, most sadly true in many cases, may come to a speedy ending; and pray for, and love your son and brother,     GEORGE."

You may be sure I got all the letters to read; and every scrap of news about my dear boy, that the little mother and her children could glean. We knew that he had won the warm approbation of his superior officers for his coolness and bravery in the battle; but not a word did we hear from him in praise of himself.

A few evenings after this letter, all the mittens were gathered together for the last time; for, as spring approached, no more could be needed, at least this winter; and all prayed, that when another cold season came round, it would be bright with peace restored all over our beloved land.

There were just twenty-one pairs. George's birthday would come on the 8th of March, when he would be of age, and they hoped that a box containing these mittens and a loving gift from each and every member of his family, would reach him in time.

"Twenty-one years old!" cried Harry. "Why, George can vote! I think that is the very best of being a man."

"So do I," said a voice at the door.

"Oh, Aunt Fanny! you little darling; come help us count up our mittens."

Down we sat, with pencils and paper, and did dreadful hard sums, the smaller ones thought, casting up the long column of mittens which had been sent to the brave soldiers. Poor Mary O'Reilly had rubbed her red bags off at last, and was sitting close to Pet, comfortably washing her face, while the "tremendous dog" winked lazily at us, to let us know that he was all right, and on our side.

How many do you guess had been made and given, beside those the little play brought? Just take the six books, turn to the last pages of each, and then count up for yourselves. It will make a very nice little sum in arithmetic.

And, my darings, it will do more, I hope, and believe. It will show you that chidren can do a great deal of good, if they only try. If I have proved this to your satisfaction, and if you should ever form or join a children's society to work for the soldiers, or help the poor, I really think you must let me know it, so that I can write you a letter, or come and give you a good, loving kiss.

And now, as my book is already getting too long, I can only tell you that George remained in his beloved General Burnside's division during the spring and summer of this year, 1862; doing his duty well, and winning the respect and love of all who knew him.

At first the General thought he was only a dandified chap, without much fighting in him, because his hair was parted so very evenly down the back of his head, and his gloves and boots were always, the one so snowy white, and the other so brilliantly black. The General did not know, as we do, that our little Johnny had given George a comb, expressly that he *might* make that very particular parting; and that his habits of scrupulous neatness in dress were a part of West Point and home education, which he would never neglect. But it was not long before the little mother's soldier son was rated as his courage and merits deserved; in proof of which he was soon writing a letter home, with the good news that he had been chosen one of the General's aids, and had had a horse given him, whose merits, in his estimation, were very little inferior to Mr. Bonner's famous horse Lantern.

\*    \*    \*    \*    \*    \*

Ah! how I grieve to part with you, my dear little readers. As I write, I always think of the sweet and bright eyes that will read, and the small hands that will hold my true story book. I wonder to myself if you have good and pure hearts; and then I pray for you all, though I do not know you, and hope that you are obedient, lovely children. Above all, I pray that no written or spoken word of mine will ever do you the least grain of harm. It would make me most wretched, did I think it possible.

Before I say good-by, I must tell you what I saw the other day, in one of the splendid show windows of Ball & Black's magnificent store.

An elegant sword and belt lay on the velvet cover, and above was a sheet of parchment with an inscription, which I went in and asked permission to copy, as I knew you would be delighted to read it. Here it is:

"Presented by the citizens of Lockport to Midshipman Benjamin H. Porter, as a testimony of their appreciation of his gallant conduct at Roanoke Island." (*We* know something about that, *don't we?*)

"Midshipman Porter was but seventeen years old, when, at the battle of Roanoke

Island, his noble daring elicited the admiration of his superior officer, who exclaimed, 'My brave boy, you have won your epaulettes!'

"He led his battery, six Dahlgren howitzers, through the swamp, and, in the face of a galling fire, continued to load and discharge one of his guns, after every man around him had been shot down; bravely remaining at his post until the enemy was dislodged and had made an unconditional surrender."

Oh! how pleased I was to see this testimony, and touch with my hand the sword that his true and brave hands would clasp.

I had just written the last word, when my little Alice's grandpapa came into the room, and handed her a package, saying, "Here, Monsieur Pop, your uncle John has sent you something by a soldier who came home wounded, and too ill to fight;" and he handed her a little parcel.

## THE ORPHAN'S HOME MITTENS. 133

This uncle was my dear brother John. He had been in some dreadful battles, and we, like all left at home, suffered constant anxiety about him, dreading that each day might bring bad news.

He had been very ill with the terrible fever, which, I believe, has killed more than the guns of the enemy, and had taken "a cartload or so" of quinine, which is the very bitterest medicine that ever was invented. It ought always to cure, it is so very bad to take. It did cure my brother; and, so far, we were grateful to know, that though foremost in the fight, no bullet had yet touched him.

So Alice eagerly took the parcel, and undid it—my father and I looking on with our eyes very wide open. Inside the first paper were three smaller parcels. She unrolled the smallest first, and out came *a little doll's china leg*, with the foot broken off.

"Why, how funny!" she exclaimed.

Then the next was quickly opened. Another little china leg, this time with a foot encased in a black gaiter boot, with a straw-colored sole to it—all painted on, of course.

The third parcel contained a china head and neck, very pretty, and quite perfect.

"Oh," cried Alice, "what a pretty doll's head! only she has no seam to her hair. It must be because she is a secession doll."

We laughed, and wondered what it meant, till we noticed that one of the papers had something written on it. They were printed pages, and seemed to be a report of something; but one of them had a blank side, and on this was written in faint pencil marks—

"CAMP NEAR HARRISON'S LANDING,
*August* 12, 1862.

"MY DEAR FATHER:
"This, with its accompanying parcel, will be handed to you by a comrade, who

has gone home ill. The parcel contains the head and legs of a porcelain doll. I picked them up last week, when out scouting with the regiment, on the right bank of the James river. They had been taken, I suppose, from one of the houses of an F. F. V., and dropped again. I found them on the estate of the Ruffin family, one of whom *fired the first gun at Sumter.*

"Give it to Alice, with my love, and let her place it in disgrace among her numerous family as 'Miss Secesh.' I will write you by mail to-day or to-morrow.

"Your affectionate son,
"JOHN."

"Oh!" said Alice, "I am sorry for the little girl that lost her doll; but I'm glad I've got it. What a good uncle John, to send it to me!"—and she immediately whirled round and made two cheeses, in honor of the event.

"How many dolls will that make?" inquired Grandpa.

"Let me see," she answered, thinking, with her finger on her lip. "Forty-one paper dolls. Then there is Willie, my small china doll; Anna, my large china doll; Baby, my wax doll, that cries, and opens and shuts its eyes; Genevieve Virginie, my new porcelain doll; and Miss Secesh.

"Bless me!" said Grandpa, "*what* a family to look after! You ought to write down the day you got Miss Secesh—twenty-fourth of August."

"No, Grandpa," said Alice, "it is the *twenty-tooth*—"

"So it is," cried Grandpa—while I had to run and look out of the window, so that the dear little old monkey should not see me laughing at her funny mistake. She meant the "twenty-second;" but you see she spoke in a hurry.

And now I must really say good-by,

my darlings, and throw my pen out of the window.

The door opens. Every one of the Little Mother's children rush in.

"What?!! what is that you say?!"

"Yes, Aunt Fanny! George is made a CAPTAIN! Hurrah!!!"

END OF THE SIXTH AND LAST BOOK.

*D. Appleton & Co.'s Publications.*

## Juvenile Works.

A PLACE FOR EVERYTHING, and EVERYTHING IN ITS PLACE. By COUSIN ALICE. 16mo, illustrated, cloth, 75 c.

AMERICAN HISTORICAL TALES. 16mo, 75 cents.

APPLETON'S BOYS' AND GIRLS' AMERICAN ANNUAL for 1860. 1 vol. 12mo, illustrated. Cloth, gilt, $1 50.

AUNT KITTY'S TALES. By MARIA J. MCINTOSH. 12mo, 75 cents.

AUNT FANNY'S STORY BOOK FOR LITTLE BOYS AND GIRLS. 18mo, illustrated, boards, 31 cents. Cloth, 38 cents.

BARON MUNCHAUSEN'S SURPRISING TRAVELS AND ADVENTURES. A new and beautiful edition. Illustrated with characteristic designs, by Crowquill. (Several colored.) 1 vol. 12mo. Extra cloth, gilt edges, $2 50.

BERTRAM NOEL. A Story for Youth. By E. J. MAY, author of "Louis' School Days," &c. 16mo, 75 cents.

BLIND ALICE. A Tale for Good Children. By MARIA J. MCINTOSH. 1 vol. square 16mo, 38 cents.

BOYS (The) AT HOME. By the author of "Edgar Clifton." 16mo, illustrated, 75 cents.

BOY'S BOOK OF MODERN TRAVEL AND ADVENTURE. By Meredith Johnes. 1 neat vol. 16mo, illustrated, cloth, 75c.

BOYS' AND GIRLS' AMERICAN ANNUAL. Edited by T. Martin. With finely colored illustrations. 1 vol. 12mo, in extra cloth, gilt edges, $1 50.

BOY'S (The) BIRTH-DAY BOOK: a Collection of Tales, Essays, and Narratives of Adventures. By Mrs. S. C. HALL, WILLIAM HOWITT, AUGUSTUS MAYHEW, THOMAS MILLER, G. A. SALA, &c., &c. 1 vol. crown 8vo, illustrated with 100 engravings. Cloth, gilt edges, $2.

BOY'S BOOK OF INDUSTRIAL INFORMATION. By ELISHA NOYCE, author of Outlines of Creation. Illustrated with 370 engravings. 12mo, extra cloth, $1 25.

BOY'S (The) OWN TOY MAKER. Square 16mo. 50 cents.

BIBLE STORIES: or, Tales from Scripture. 1 vol. square 12mo.

BOY'S OWN BOOK: a Complete Encyclopædia of all the Diversions, Athletic, Scientific, and Recreative, of Boyhood and Youth. New and enlarged edition, with numerous additional illustrations. 1 thick vol., extra cloth, $2.

*D. Appleton & Co.'s Publications.*

## Juvenile Works.

CHILDREN'S HOLIDAYS. A Story Book for the whole Year. 18mo, illustrated. Cloth, 50 cents.

CHILD'S FIRST HISTORY OF AMERICA. By the author of "Little Dora." Square 18mo, engravings. Half cloth, 25 cents.

CHILDREN'S (The) PICTURE GALLERY. Engravings from one hundred paintings by eminent English artists. 1 vol. 4to, $1 50.

DOUGLASS FARM. A Juvenile Story of Life in Virginia. By MARY E. BRADLEY. 16mo, illustrated. Cloth, 75 cents.

EDGAR CLIFTON; or, RIGHT and WRONG. 16mo. Illus. 75 cents.

ELLEN LESLIE; or, the REWARD of SELF-CONTROL. By MARIA J. McINTOSH. 1 vol. square 16mo, 38 cents.

EMILY HERBERT; or, THE HAPPY HOME. By MARIA J. McINTOSH. 1 vol. square 12mo, 38 cents.

ENTOMOLOGY in SPORT and ENTOMOLOGY in EARNEST. By Two Lovers of the Science. 1 vol. 12mo. $1 25.

FAGGOTS for THE FIRESIDE; or, FACTS and FANCY. By Peter Parley. 1 vol. 12mo, beautifully illustrated, $1 12.

FLORENCE ARNOTT; or, IS SHE GENEROUS? By MARIA J. McINTOSH. 1 vol. square 16mo, 38 cents.

FUNNY STORY BOOK; A LAUGHTER PROVOKING BOOK FOR YOUNG FOLKS. 16mo, illustrated, cloth, 75c. Extra cloth, gilt edges, $1.

GEORGE READY; or, HOW TO LIVE FOR OTHERS. By ROBERT O'LINCOLN. 16mo, illustrated. Cloth, 75 cents.

GOOD IN EVERY THING. By Mrs. BARWELL. Square 16mo, illustrated, 50 cents.

GRACE AND CLARA; or, BE JUST, as WELL AS GENEROUS. 1 vol. square 16mo, 38 cents.

GRANDMAMMA EASY'S TOY BOOKS. 8vo. colored. Per dozen, $1 50.

HEWET'S ILLUMINATED HOUSEHOLD STORIES FOR LITTLE FOLKS. Beautifully illustrated.

  No. 1. CINDERELLA,
  " 2. JACK THE GIANT KILLER.
  " 3. PUSS IN BOOTS.
  " 4. LITTLE RED RIDING HOOD.
  " 5. JACK AND THE BEAN STALK.
  " 6. TOM THUMB.
  " 7. BEAUTY AND THE BEAST. In fancy paper covers, each 25 cents. In fancy boards, each 50 cents.

## Juvenile Books.

HISTORY OF PETER THE GREAT, CZAR OF RUSSIA. By SARAH H. BRADFORD. 16mo, illustrated, cloth, 75 cents.

HOUSEHOLD STORIES. Collected by the Brothers GRIMM Newly translated, embellished with 240 illustrations by Wehnert. 1 vol., cloth, $2 00. Gilt edges, $2 50.

HOWITT'S (MARY), SERIES of POPULAR JUVENILE WORKS. 14 vols. uniform, in a case, in extra cloth, neat style.

HOWITT'S (MARY), PICTURE AND VERSE BOOK, commonly called Otto Speckter's Fable Book. Illustrated with 100 plates. Cheap edition, 50 cents. Cloth, 68 cents. Gilt leaves, 75 cents.

JESSIE GRAHAM; or, FRIENDS DEAR, BUT TRUTH DEARER. By MARIA J. McINTOSH. 1 vol., square 16mo, 88 cents.

LITTLE DORA; or, THE FOUR SEASONS. By a Lady of Charleston. Beautifully illustrated, 25 cents. Cloth, 38 cents.

LITTLE FRANK, and other TALES. Square 16mo. Cloth, 25 cents.

LOSS AND GAIN; or, MARGARET'S HOME. By COUSIN ALICE.

LOUIS' SCHOOL DAYS. By E. J. MAY. Illustrated 16mo. 75 cents.

LOUISE; or, THE BEAUTY OF INTEGRITY, and other TALES. 16mo, boards, 25 cents. Cloth, 38 cents.

McINTOSH'S NEW JUVENILE LIBRARY. 7 beautiful vols. With illustrations. In a case, $2 50.

——————— META GRAY; or, What Makes HOME HAPPY? 16mo, cloth.

MARY LEE. A Story for the Young. By KATE LIVERMORE. 1 neat vol. 16mo, illustrated. Extra Cloth, 63 cents.

MARTHA'S HOOKS and EYES. 1 vol. 18mo, 87 cents.

MARRYATT'S SETTLERS IN CANADA. 2 vols. in one, colored, 62 cents.

——————— SCENES IN AFRICA. 2 vols. in one, colored 62 cents.

——————— MASTERMAN READY. 8 vols in one, colored. $2 cents.

*D. Appleton & Co.'s Publications.*

## Juvenile Books.

MIDSUMMER FAYS: or, THE HOLIDAYS at WOODLEIGH. By SUSAN PINDAR. 1 vol. 16mo, 63 cents.

MORTIMER'S COLLEGE LIFE. With neat illustrations, 16mo, cloth, 75 cents. Extra cloth, gilt edges, $1.

MYSTERIOUS STORY BOOK; or, the GOOD STEPMOTHER. Illustrated, 16mo, cloth, 75 cents. Gilt edges, $1.

NEAL (ALICE B.) CONTENTMENT Better than WEALTH. 16mo, illustrated, 63 cents. Gilt edges, 90 cents.

—————— PATIENT WAITING NO LOSS. 16mo, illustrated, 63 cents. Gilt edges, 90 cents.

—————— NO SUCH WORD AS FAIL. 16mo, illustrated, 63 cents. Gilt edges, 90 cents.

—————— "ALL'S NOT GOLD that GLITTERS," or, the YOUNG CALIFORNIAN. 1 vol. 16mo, neatly illustrated, 75 cents. Gilt edges, $1.

—————— NOTHING VENTURE, NOTHING HAVE. 1 vol. 16mo, beautifully illustrated, 63 cents. Gilt edges, 90 cents.

—————— OUT OF DEBT, OUT OF DANGER. 16mo, illustrated, cloth, 75 cents. Gilt edges, $1.

—————— A PLACE for EVERYTHING. 16mo, cloth, 75 cents

—————— THE COOPERS, or, GETTING UNDER WAY. 12mo, cloth, 75 cents.

NIGHT CAPS. By the author of "Aunt Fanny's Christmas Stories." 1 vol. 18mo, cloth, 50 cents.

NIGHT CAPS (The New). Told to Charley. By the author of "Aunt Fanny's Christmas Stories."

OUTLINES OF CREATION. By ELISHA NOYCE, author of "The Boy's Book of Industrial Information." 12mo, profusely illustrated, extra cloth, $1 50.

PARLEY'S PRESENT for ALL SEASONS. By S. G. GOODRICH, (Peter Parley.) Illustrated with 16 fine engravings. 12mo, elegantly bound in a new style, $1. Gilt edges, $1 25.

PELL'S GUIDE for THE YOUNG to Success and Happiness. 12mo, cloth, 38 cents. Extra cloth, gilt edges, 50 cents.

PHILIP RANDOLPH. A Tale of Virginia. By MARY GERTRUDE. 18mo, 38 cents.

PICTURE PLEASURE BOOK (The). Illustrated by upwards of five hundred engravings from drawings by eminent artists. 4to. size, beautifully printed, on fine paper, and bound in fancy covers. First and Second Series, each $1 25.

## Juvenile Books.

PUSS IN BOOTS. Finely illustrated by Otto Speckter. Square 18mo, boards, 25 cents. Cloth, 38 cents. Extra gilt, 50 cents.

ROBINSON CRUSOE. Pictorial edition. 300 plates, 8vo, $1 50. Gilt edges, $2.

ROSE and LILLIE STANHOPE; or, THE POWER of CONSCIENCE. By MARIA J. McINTOSH. 1 vol., 38 cents.

SEDGEMOOR; or, HOME LESSONS. By Mrs. MANNERS. 16mo. Cloth, 75 cents.

STORIES of an OLD MAID. By Madame DE GIRARDIN. 16mo, Illustrated, cloth, 75 cents.

SUNSHINE of GREYSTONE. By the author of "Louis' School Days." 16mo, illustrated, 75 cents.

UNCLE JOHN'S FIRST BOOK. Illustrated with numerous pretty engravings. Square 16mo, neat cloth, 31 cents.

UNCLE JOHN'S SECOND BOOK. Illustrated with numerous pretty engravings. Square 18mo, in neat cloth, 38 cents.

VICAR OF WAKEFIELD. A Tale. By OLIVER GOLDSMITH. 1 vol, 12mo, with numerous illustrations, 75 cents. Gilt edges.

WANDERERS (The): by SEA and LAND, with Other Tales. By Peter Parley. Illustrated with exquisite designs. 1 vol. 12mo. $1 12.

THE WEEK'S DELIGHT; or, GAMES and STORIES for the PARLOR and FIRESIDE. 1 neat volume. 16mo, engravings. 75 cents.

WILLIAM TELL, The PATRIOT OF SWITZERLAND: to which is added, Andreas Hofer, the "Tell" of the Tyrol. Cloth, 50 cents. Half cloth, 38 cents.

A WINTER WREATH of SUMMER FLOWERS. By S. G. GOODRICH. Illustrated with splendid colored plates by French artists. 1 superb vol. 8vo, extra cloth, gilt edges, $3.

YOUNG STUDENT (The); or, RALPH and VICTOR. By Madame GUIZOT. From the French, by Samuel Jackson. 1 vol. of 500 pages, with illustrations, 75 cents.

YOUTH'S CORONAL. By H. F. GOULD, 16mo, 63 cents.

———— STORY BOOK. 16mo, 75 cents.

*D. Appleton & Co.'s Publications.*

## MINIATURE CLASSICAL LIBRARY.
PUBLISHED IN ELEGANT FORM, WITH FRONTISPIECES.

| | |
|---|---|
| Poetic Lacon; or, Aphorisms from the Poets | $0 38 |
| Bond's Golden Maxims | 31 |
| Clarke's Scripture Promises. Complete | 38 |
| Elizabeth; or, the Exiles of Siberia | 31 |
| Goldsmith's Vicar of Wakefield | 38 |
| ——— Essays | 38 |
| Gems from American Poets | 38 |
| Hannah More's Private Devotions | 31 |
| ——— Practical Piety. 2 vols | 75 |
| Hemans' Domestic Affections | 31 |
| Hoffman's Lays of the Hudson, &c. | 38 |
| Johnson's History of Rasselas | 38 |
| Manual of Matrimony | 31 |
| Moore's Lalla Rookh | 38 |
| ——— Melodies. Complete | 38 |
| Paul and Virginia | 31 |
| Pollok's Course of Time | 38 |
| Pure Gold from the Rivers of Wisdom | 38 |
| Thomson's Seasons | 38 |
| Token of the Heart. Do. of Affections. Do. of Remembrance. Do. of Love. Do. of Friendship. (5 vols.) Each | 31 |
| Useful Letter-Writer | 38 |
| Wilson's Sacra Privata | 31 |
| Young's Night Thoughts | 38 |

www.ingramcontent.com/pod-product-compliance
Lightning Source LLC
Chambersburg PA
CBHW031455160426
43195CB00010BB/987